STRAIGHT
FROM THE

STRAIGHT
FROM THE
Heart

*An Essential Guide
for Developing,
Deepening, and
Renewing Your
Relationships*

Layne & Paul
CUTRIGHT

HEART TO HEART • SAN DIEGO, CALIFORNIA

Heart to Heart
7720-B El Camino Real
Suite 441
La Costa, CA 92009

First edition 1996

Designed and typeset by Robert Mott and Kathy Wise for
    Robert Mott & Associates
Edited by Deena Tuttle for Just Write

Printed in the United States of America

ISBN: 0-9651371-0-4

The main text of this book is typeset in Calligraphic 810. The subheads are typeset in Calligraphic 810 with beginning caps typeset in Flemish Script.

How Do You Know This Is the Right Book For You?

ASK YOURSELF THESE QUESTIONS
AND CHECK THE ONES TO WHICH YOU ANSWER YES.

❑ Do I avoid talking about things I know I should because
I'm afraid it will hurt someone's feelings?

❑ Do I find it hard to say "I love you" or to express affection
and acknowledgment verbally?

❑ Do I get uncomfortable receiving attention?

❑ Do I deflect praise and compliments by downplaying them?

❑ Do I "bite my tongue" again and again rather than speak my
mind, until I finally blow up at someone?

❑ Do I get uncomfortable when someone is expressing intense
emotion?

❑ Do I avoid necessary confrontations?

❑ Has anyone ever told me that I just don't listen?

❑ Do I have trouble setting and honoring boundaries in my
relationships?

❑ Do I wish I felt more loved by the people I know love me?

❑ Do I find it hard to express how I really feel?

❑ Do I have a hard time receiving "constructive criticism"?

❑ Do I ever feel like people don't listen to me?

❑ Do I ever feel like I want more out of my relationships, but
I don't know how to get it?

❑ Do I have trouble asking for what I want?

❑ Have I ever been hurt by "the truth"?

❑ Have I ever wanted to say something important and had it come out all wrong?

Honestly, if you answered yes to even one of these questions, you can benefit from reading *Straight From the Heart*. Reading this book and doing the processes in it will help you to

- feel heard and understood,
- feel closer and more connected with others,
- feel safer in your relationships,
- be yourself,
- feel more confident and competent in your relationships,
- say what you mean,
- mean what you say,
- really listen to others,
- feel loved and cared for,
- feel nurtured and empowered,
- be authentic,
- ask for what you want,
- get what you want.

# $\mathcal{D}$EDICATION

This book is dedicated to all those people

who not only know love

is the most important thing in life,

but who also live like it.

Acknowledgments

We want to express our gratitude and appreciation for some of the people who have loved and supported us all along the way, holding the banner of faith for us when ours was flagging.

Sally Rorick-Orlando—for being our right hand day in and day out over the last seven years, for her strength and tenderness, for loving us and believing in us, and for holding the vision through all the ups and downs.

Pamela and William Noyes—for being the best friends anyone could ever want to have, for their abundant loving and unconditional support, and for living the essence of this book and sharing a path of spiritual adventure with us.

Benedict St. Germain, Layne's mother—for initiating me into the realm of unconditional love. The life I live is built upon the loving foundation she provided. I am forever thankful.

Jessie Irene Kirk, Paul's mother—for always loving me and encouraging me to follow my heart, and for teaching me to always be true to myself. From my childhood I remember her often quoting me Shakespeare's couplet, "This above all: to thine own self be true...."

Rama, Paul's father—for declaring to me in my early twenties that I was no longer his son, but now forever his brother. He taught me that I am more than any role I may perform in life and that we are all equally beloved children of our creator.

Deena Tuttle—for her uncanny ability to capture our thoughts and intentions and helping give them expression in this book, and for the generosity of spirit she brought to our work together.

Karen Risch—for her love and encouragement in this and all our writing projects, and for always relating with us straight from the heart.

Robert Mott—for designing this book with excellence and love, for his abundant generosity and belief in our vision, and for going out of his way to make this project possible.

We want to acknowledge the following people for their contributions to this project and for making the world a better place by sharing what they have learned with so much love and enthusiasm: Terry and Ken Courian, Vikki and Gary Goodman, Linda Greenwell, Deborah and Sidney Haygood, Joe Manning, Nancy Patterson and Jim Kinney, Debbe and Michael Simmons, Kathryn Taylor and Al Curtice, Tina and Mark Terry, and Cora Van Loon and Bob Battaglia.

We also want to acknowledge all the graduates of the Accelerated Personal Empowerment Program for honoring the vision of a new way to live, for their courage in stepping onto the path, and for their trust in themselves and us by joining in the experiment of Evolutionary Relationships.

$\mathscr{C}$ONTENTS

Introduction 1

PART ONE: TRUTH IS LOVE'S DOORWAY

    1. The Healing Power of Truth 9

    2. Telling the Truth 17

    3. Hearing the Truth 27

    4. Dealing with the Truth 35

PART TWO: STEPPING THROUGH THE OPEN DOOR

    5. How to Have Heart-to-Heart Talks 49

    6. Building Friendship 69

    7. Discovering the Self 75

    8. Forgiveness and Healing Hurts 83

    9. Deepening Intimacy and Trust 89

    10. Bonding with Family .95

    11. Enhancing Ties with Co-Workers 101

    12. Creating Love and Romance 107

    13. Sharing Power and Co-Creation 113

    14. Windows of the Soul .121

    15. A New Way of Living .125

One cannot be strong without love.

For love is not an irrelevant emotion;

it is the blood of life,

the power of reunion of the separated.

PAUL TILLICH

$\mathscr{I}$NTRODUCTION

Gentle Reader,

We have written this book to share with you a magical and
powerful tool you can use to bring more love, trust, intimacy,
joy, heartfelt soul connection, excitement, growth, and
adventure into your life and relationships than you may ever
have thought possible. Nothing is more important than your
relationships, because your relationships affect every part of
your life. We think you'll agree it is in relationships your
deepest feelings arise. Your relationships can take you from the
depths of hurt, disappointment, rage, and grief to the heights
of joy, love, anticipation, and ecstasy—sometimes all in the

same day and all within one relationship! There is no question that relating with our fellow human beings can sometimes be heartwarming and magical and at other times tedious and agonizing. The fact is most problems in relationships are born of misunderstanding and miscommunication.

As individuals we live on our own solitary islands of reality, absorbed in and fascinated by our own points of view. Frequently we reach out to one another seeking to understand or be understood. The bridge between our separate realities is communication. Communication is what joins us with others. To communicate is to relate; without communication of some kind there is no relationship. To a very large degree the quality of your relationships depends upon the quality of your communication. And it is the breakdowns in communication that often generate the heartbreak and disappointment of unfulfilled dreams, visions, and goals.

The most treasured moments in our lives occur when we as individuals connect from the heart with the soul of someone else. Most people experience this rarely, if ever. What we have discovered is that these moments of true connection can be deliberately created. Using the principles and processes in this book you will develop the skill to fill your life with these kinds of moments. You will be reawakened to your capacity to connect deeply with the people you care about most in an upwelling of compassion.

As individuals we live on our own solitary islands of reality, absorbed in and fascinated by our own points of view.

"What is one of the biggest challenges you have in your relationships?" we often ask participants in our workshops. What we hear over and over again is, "Communication!"

Most people have a lot of frustration and confusion associated with communication. They recognize that they need to talk about some difficult issues but often don't know how to bring them up. Nor do they trust their ability to navigate through the rough spots to honest, heartfelt resolution for everyone concerned. Some people talk incessantly, as if in a desperate attempt to be heard and validated, but instead end up driving people away. Others are very closed and secretive, as if they are afraid of being found out somehow. Still others seem to blame everything wrong in their lives on others, then wonder why they feel isolated and alone. Some people never seem to listen, but are always quick either to talk about themselves or to offer unsolicited advice.

Do you do any of these things in your relationships? Do you know anyone who does? When someone is speaking to you, are you so busy thinking about what you want to say that sometimes you don't even hear the other person?

Do you feel safe letting people know when you are afraid or insecure, or do you think you are supposed to appear strong and in control to be loved or respected? Can you talk freely about the things that are truly important to you, as well as the things that bother you, or are you afraid of appearing vulnerable and foolish?

What if you felt totally at ease and comfortable being your true, authentic self in your relationships with others? What do you think would happen if you felt safe enough to tell the truth about your thoughts and feelings all the time in your relationships? What if others felt safe enough to tell *you* the truth about their thoughts and feelings? How do you think you would feel about each other? Our experience with our students and clients has shown over and over again that they end up feeling closer and more trusting with each other. There is a direct correlation between honesty, intimacy, and trust.

Have you ever told someone you care about that you want to have a "heart-to-heart talk"? For most people, having a *heart to heart* implies there is some truth or feeling to share. It could be any of a number of things: an expression of love and acknowledgment, a request for (or offer of) advice or counsel on a sensitive matter, or, just as easily, a problem or an upset. In all cases a request for a heart-to-heart talk implies value to the relationship and a certain level of existing trust.

Outside the context of such conversations, however, problems arise all too frequently in relationships because of miscommunication and misunderstanding. Feelings get hurt; there is anger, sadness, and defensiveness. The walls go up, and usually there is no further discussion. Over time love becomes more of a concept than a feeling. ("Why, of course I love you. Don't be silly!") Trust diminishes, and real intimacy is lost.

Usually when people are having problems and misunderstandings, they tend to think there is something wrong with them, or the other person, or both. The more disappointments you have over time, the more this attitude is reinforced. We have a different point of view, however. What we have discovered is that people have problems and misunderstandings in their relationships not because there is something wrong with them, but rather because they lack education in the fundamental principles and practices of successful relationships. If you approach relationship challenges with the attitude there is something to learn—and you *can* learn it—as opposed to the attitude that there is something wrong with you that needs fixing, then your chances of producing successful relationships are greatly increased.

One of the most important skills to learn and practice in relationships is the art of successful communication. When you practice effective, satisfying communication you are rewarded with relationships filled with more love, understanding, trust, and intimacy.

The processes you will learn with this book are called Heart-to-Heart Talks. They have been tested and proven effective with thousands of people, beginning with ourselves. We know these processes work from our own personal experience in creating, nurturing, developing, and growing our own relationship. When we first got together in 1976, we acknowledged that we

Approach relationship challenges with the attitude there is something to learn— and you can learn it.

5

were going to have to do a lot of things differently than we had in the past if we expected our relationship to last. It quickly became clear that one of the most important areas to pay attention to was communication. The exercises you will learn and use in this book are some of the same processes we used.

Part One of this book will provide you with a firm foundation for thoroughly understanding and using these powerful processes. Part Two will explain the principles, lay out the guidelines, then offer the step-by-step processes for conducting Heart-to-Heart Talks. So be patient, and do not rush too quickly to the processes until you have grasped all that is in Part One.

We wish you all that you desire from your relationships. Thank you for the opportunity to accompany you along your journey there.

LAYNE AND PAUL CUTRIGHT

PART ONE

TRUTH IS LOVE'S DOORWAY

The absolute value of love makes life
worthwhile and so makes man's
strange and difficult situation acceptable.
Love cannot save life from death,
but it can fulfill life's purpose.

ARNOLD TOYNBEE

CHAPTER ONE

THE HEALING POWER
OF TRUTH

Telling the truth is a phrase that can unleash an avalanche of emotions from fear to desperation to hopefulness. Sometimes when people think about telling the whole truth their breath gets shallow, their stomach seizes up, their palms sweat, and their mouth gets dry.

Why does the idea of telling the truth stir such deep concern? Usually it comes from our childhood training about the truth. Too often children are told with a threatening tone, "You'd better tell the truth now!" or "Who did this?!" Or perhaps our siblings and classmates tattled on us, getting us into trouble. Again and again the truth is used as a weapon to hurt us. It seems quite logical to decide that the truth hurts.

The problem is we bring this decision into our adult lives, where it creates walls in our relationships. We live and communicate as though our truth is unacceptable, even harmful, to others and that it is dangerous to reveal. We censor. We edit. We avoid. This fear makes enemies of our loved ones. It turns relationships that should be an oasis of love, safety, and encouragement into just another place we have to protect ourselves. It turns our loving relationships into yet another battleground. What a sorrowful thing this is, especially when it doesn't have to be that way!

GIVING AND RECEIVING LOVE

Truth can be healing. Truth can be a doorway to a greater experience of love than you have ever known. Truth can heal the past and free your future. Truth can bring you peace. Truth can help you love and respect yourself more fully. Truth can tear down the walls of separation that isolate you from your loved ones. Truth can build understanding and compassion. Truth can make you whole.

How can it do this? you might ask. When you live life with a secret self—a self you feel is unacceptable and unlovable—you destroy your ability to feel loved. You may *know* you are loved, but you won't *feel* loved.

Relationships with a history gather a storehouse of unspoken hurts, disappointments, and misinterpretations that lead to the heart closing down. When difficult events occurred we rationalized in some way; we told ourselves they weren't important enough to talk about or that talking about them wouldn't do any good. Yet if closeness is important to you, this is dangerous thinking: Over time, these unspoken concerns gather mass, gradually weakening the connection we feel. To renew a longtime relationship there is nothing more effective than having a good Heart-to-Heart Talk to clear the air and revitalize the love.

Right now, think of just two people who are important to you and ask yourself, "Is there anything I've been afraid to tell them?" What comes to mind? There is a big chance that those things are in the way of deeper, more satisfying relationships.

Your truth is part of you. When you feel your truth is unacceptable, you feel *you* are unacceptable. Then love becomes an enemy. Why? Because love is a great healer. Love brings up anything unlike itself. When someone loves you unconditionally, it can stir up deep, hidden feelings of being unacceptable, your fear of being "found out": You feel that if they really knew what you were about, they wouldn't love you! Those feelings can be very strong, even overpowering. They can even make you feel a little crazy.

Love
brings up
anything
unlike itself.

11

There you are, sharing love with someone, and all of a sudden you feel like crying or running away.

As the closely guarded and buried wounds around your heart start to be revealed to your conscious awareness, you feel vulnerable, at risk. If you don't have any experience with the healing power of love, the smart thing to do seems to be to get away from this discomfort, to hide yourself from the love. There are certainly many ways of deflecting love; in fact, you have probably become an expert at doing this. Which ways do you prefer? Changing the subject? Eating? Smoking? Drinking? Watching TV? Picking a fight? Getting sick? Spending more time at work? Doing things you know will irritate people so they won't love you so much? Going numb? Being emotionally unavailable? Becoming a complainer and fault finder?

But what would happen if you understood the healing power of love and how it works? By far, the best thing is to keep letting the love in and allow your feelings to surface. *Seize the healing opportunity. Surrender to the moment. Lose control.* Only by doing this can you heal your emotional pain. Allow the wound to be opened even more. Let yourself express the feelings you've held onto so tightly. Let go! Love washes away the fear, the hurt, the guilt, the anger.

Keep letting go. Love is a balm that soothes and heals the wounds of the heart. By letting it in you will rediscover your true self. You will feel purged and refreshed. You will feel closer

Love is a balm that soothes and heals the wounds of the heart. By letting it in you will rediscover your true self.

to your loved ones. You will have expanded your capacity
to receive and give love. You will feel safe and more deeply
understood. You will experience greater trust in yourself and
with others. You will be happier. You will be healed.

THE FOUR PRINCIPLES OF HEART-TO-HEART TALKS

There is no question that it takes courage to tell the truth
and let love work its magic. What's more, the process doesn't
happen all at once. It happens bit by bit. The more you do it,
the safer it feels. The safer it feels, the more you do it, and so on.

In the early stages of our relationship when we were dating
we would invent processes to do for the purpose of learning
about each other: how we thought, how we felt, what was
important to each of us. Later, when we were living together, we
never went to bed at night without doing two communication
processes. This enabled us to build a strong foundation of trust,
understanding, and openness.

Most important during this time, we had an agreement
always to tell each other the truth about our thoughts and
feelings. Of course, that was not always an easy thing to do.
Sometimes it was really scary, especially when we were afraid
our thoughts and feelings were unacceptable or would hurt

each other. But because we knew how important it was, we continued to honor our commitment always to be honest with each other.

You see, we thought of our relationship as an experiment. We weren't always sure of what we were doing in those days. All we knew was that the way we had done it in the past had not worked. We both had a history of painful, broken relationships. There was no reason to believe this relationship would work any better than any of our others. We did have love going for us, but we had long since learned that love by itself is not enough to guarantee success in a relationship. The one thing that was different was we were willing to experiment in our relationship and try new things, all based on the premise that *we could create our relationship exactly the way we wanted it.*

Of all the things we experimented with twenty years ago in creating our relationship, the communication processes in this book—Heart-to-Heart Talks—were among the most important. When we first began practicing Heart-to-Heart Talks, we used them within the context of four principles. First, we acknowledge that all human beings are more alike than different. We all need food, clothing, and a warm, dry place to live. We all want to be valued and appreciated. We all need to feel connected to others in a community of support and acceptance. We all want to know that our being here is a contribution in some way to others. Any differences that exist based upon gender, race, or culture, profound as they may be, are secondary to our common humanity. When we enter into relationships acknowledging our common humanity, the differences become much easier to tolerate and accommodate—even appreciate.

Second, we affirm that the essence of all human beings is love. What is essential in all of us is not visible to the eye, but can only be perceived by the eye of the heart. This requires the ability, or at least the willingness, to see beyond others' fears and limitations into their very heart of hearts. Regardless of the hardships or abuses that anyone has suffered, there is an untouched purity of spirit that may be brought forth simply by being recognized and acknowledged.

The third principle is the crux of this book. When fears are shared in a space of loving kindness, with the intention to release them, they diminish and even disappear. When love is expressed in a space of acceptance, it grows stronger. This leads to a direct experience of our common essence.

The fourth principle we followed is perhaps the most radical of all. It says that we are all responsible for our own feelings. There is no room for blame or playing the victim with this principle. This, perhaps more than anything else, helped us to become impeccable observers of our own deeply felt beliefs and reactions. Our commitment was to speak and behave as if this principle were true, even (and especially) if it didn't feel like

The essence
of all
human beings
is love.

it. If we felt like blaming each other or defending ourselves against a perceived attack, that was a signal to begin looking within. *Unless someone is speaking with the intention to hurt, the pain we feel is in fact an already existing hurt from the past that has simply been triggered by what was said.* This is one of the most essential principles to comprehend if you are to use your relationships for learning, healing, and growth.

Our consistent practice of Heart-to-Heart Talks formed the foundation upon which we built our relationship, and we have since taught them to thousands of people who have used them with similar success. We offer these exercises in telling the truth to you now for your own experiment in creating extraordinary relationships.

Truth can be a healer or a destroyer. If truth can be such a powerful tool for good or ill, then it becomes very important to learn more about how it works so you can wield this double-edged sword with skill and finesse. It becomes imperative to know how to speak the truth, hear the truth, and deal with the truth. Read on, and we'll show you how!

CHAPTER TWO

TELLING
THE TRUTH

A word of caution: When we talk about telling the truth, we mean the truth of your thoughts and feelings, especially those thoughts and feelings you think are not acceptable or that, if known, will cause you to lose love. We are not suggesting you begin by confessing your major transgressions against another person, such as the affair you had last year. Although the processes in this book are perfectly capable of guiding you through such deep waters, we strongly recommend that you use them with smaller issues at first. If you have deeper, more potentially devastating issues to deal with, we urge you to seek professional support. Certainly your familiarity with the principles and practices in this book will aid you immeasurably in any work you may do with a therapist or counselor.

WHAT WE LEARNED FROM OUR FAMILIES

What was communication like in your family when you were growing up? Was it easy to talk to each other about things that were important to you, such as people and things you loved, or things that made you sad or angry? Could you talk about your disappointments and hurts? Was it easy to express your excitement and enthusiasm? Was there tolerance for differing opinions? Did you feel heard and understood by your parents? Were they affectionate and demonstrative with you and with each other? Did they really listen to each other?

Or did you experience a lot of shouting in your family? Did you get the message that it was taboo to talk about feelings? Was it common to deal with issues by keeping silent about them, then letting things gradually return to "normal," as if nothing had ever happened? Did you ever feel there was something you were always trying to get across to your parents when you were growing up, such as, "Listen to me!" or "Pay attention to me!" or "Leave me alone!" or "You just don't care!" or "You don't understand me!" or "Please, just love me!"?

The way people communicated in your family is probably the way you tend to communicate now. You also tend to attract people who are consistent with whatever your family's communication style was. For instance, if you got the silent treatment a lot when you were growing up, you will likely attract someone who is uncommunicative and distant. It's also possible that if shouting was the norm in your family, but you never had the experience of being heard, you may attract someone who is uncommunicative and distracted so you still feel you are not being heard. The tendency is to recreate the feeling you had as a child growing up. So you find yourself saying the same or similar things in your adult relationships that you were trying to communicate to your parents, such as, "Why don't you ever listen to me!" or "You never pay any attention to me anymore!" or "Leave me alone!" or "You just don't care about me!" or "You just don't understand me!"

Many people, when they grow up, say they aren't going to be anything like their parents. They go to great lengths not to be like them, and it may work for a while. But because of the power of modeling, eventually they end up behaving and responding just like their parents in ways of which they are unaware, despite their best efforts to the contrary. Another problem is that in our society today, most of us are under stress most of the time—and the times our communication style is most like our parents' is when we are under stress. That's when we find ourselves saying things our mother or father might have said in just the way they might have said it, because it is the way we learned to do it.

> You will tend to recreate the feeling you had as a child growing up.

Heart-to-Heart Talks offer you a new way to communicate and relate with others. You can have the experience of being heard and understood by the people you love, and you can provide that same experience for your partner and others in your life who are important to you. This book will show you how. With Heart-to-Heart Talks, you can:

- ❧ Clear up misunderstandings
- ❧ Heal emotional pain
- ❧ Build intimacy
- ❧ Build trust and safety
- ❧ Build inner strength
- ❧ Change problems into growth opportunities
- ❧ Generate more self-acceptance
- ❧ Create richer relationships
- ❧ Feel emotionally stronger and freer
- ❧ Feel more connected with others
- ❧ Release tension from relationships
- ❧ Create strong, healthy relationships that empower each person to make a greater contribution to society

Absolute Musts for Telling the Truth

When you tell the truth, the first step is to know the intention of your communication. This is very important because *your intention determines your results.* If your intention is to create healing, intimacy, more harmony or more clarity, that's what will happen. If your intention is to make the other person "wrong" and yourself "right," you will generate distrust and a struggle for power. If your intention is to hurt or seek revenge, you will build walls and contribute to an emotional environment that inhibits or works against closeness and trust.

The second step is to determine beforehand how well the listener will handle the truth. Does the person tend to take everything personally? Is there a history of spite, abuse, or betrayal in the relationship? Is this person good at keeping secrets? Does this person show caring and helpfulness with you?

Your mate may or may not be an appropriate person with whom to start telling the truth. Of course, it is important to be honest with your mate, because there is a direct relationship between honesty and intimacy—the more honesty there is, the more intimacy there is. But if your mate has a tendency toward blame or attack, it is best to save your truth telling with this person for a later time, after you have built trust in the healing power of truth and have a better handle on the fundamentals. Other appropriate people to start sharing your truth with can be those in support groups and personal growth classes, counselors, and therapists. Counselors and therapists are usually ideal because they have already been trained to listen to others' truth without being judgmental and are less apt to take things personally than other people in your life. The most important thing is to get started *now* with someone.

By telling the truth you are creating a new foundation from which to live your life. Rather than operating as though you must hide your true self or that you are bad and unacceptable and can't trust the people you love, you will proceed as though your loved ones are allies who contribute to your self-acceptance through understanding, forgiveness, and love.

This can seem impossible to some people, too good to be true to others. But with our experience of leading thousands of people through Heart-to-Heart Talks, we can promise you unequivocally that *if you begin the process and learn your lessons well, you will succeed.* There isn't any great mystery about this process. It is so predictable as to be downright scientific. It requires an understanding of the human heart and the human mind, something anyone with sufficient interest can attain. *That means you.* You wouldn't be reading this book if you weren't interested. So, even if it seems impossible, it's not. Even if it seems too good to be true, it's not.

As you embark on this process, it is important to be aware of the fears you will meet and inevitably triumph over. This is the third step: Be aware of your fears about telling the truth. It's easier to overcome an enemy you can see and call by name than one that is hidden, cloaked in darkness, and unknown to you.

Have no doubt fear is your biggest enemy at this stage. Most people's fears about telling the truth are that they will be hurt or will hurt someone's feelings, or that they will be judged or misunderstood. Sometimes it's just because they don't like feeling vulnerable or out of control.

Whatever fears you have, they probably have a bigger bark than bite. Fears appear much bigger than they really are. Realize not only are you bigger than your fears, but also most often the source of the fear is within you, not something or someone outside of you. The fear is usually caused by a belief developed from an experience in your past. The fear you feel in your body is only flowing from a memory, not any real or present danger.

This is a time for courage. Courage is not something you need when you feel safe; courage is what you need when you are afraid. Courage is what it takes to feel your fear and continue anyway. The idea that helped us face our fears as we created our relationship was to consider truth-telling an experiment: Would it work? How well would it work? We were astonished by the positive results. In a nutshell, *know your fear, feel your fear, and proceed anyway*.

It is difficult to describe the sense of freedom and peace that comes from breaking through fears to tell the truth. But once you have experienced this dimension of truth telling in your relationships, you will never want to settle for less.

Usually your fear about telling the truth can be traced to your past.

The fourth step in speaking your truth is to release your need to be agreed with. Too many people require the security of knowing they will be agreed with before they speak their mind, and this works against them. The goal is to stand in your own truth, even when you do have some fear, regardless of whether people will agree with you or not. It is good to remember here that personal truth is an evolving thing. It grows and changes. Often when one person shares his or her truth and listens to the truth of another, something new comes out of their conversation. There is a new and higher level of truth born of their speaking that never could have happened if they had been waiting for the safety of agreement before they spoke.

The fifth step in telling the truth is to begin practicing and keep practicing. Select the person or persons with whom you are going to share your truth. As we mentioned earlier, for some people it's easier to begin with someone who is not personally involved, such as a classmate in a personal growth seminar, or a support group member, or a therapist or counselor. Even though the fears may make you feel uncomfortable temporarily, they won't be so strong as to overpower you and prevent you from receiving the benefit of the healing power of truth. Practice builds confidence. The more you do it, the easier it gets.

FIVE STEPS
FOR TELLING THE TRUTH

1. Know the intention of your communication.

2. Determine beforehand how well the listener will handle the truth.

3. Be aware of your fears about telling the truth.

4. Release your need to be agreed with.

5. Begin practicing, and keep practicing!

As you will learn in Part Two, there are four basic kinds of processes that make up Heart-to-Heart Talks. Select three with which to get started. Don't be misled by their simplicity; they are extremely potent, so don't overdo it. It's better to start small and work up rather than start too big and overwhelm yourself.

To do the process, pick a time when you know you will not be disturbed. You may want to start by talking about your own fears of telling the whole truth. This can have a very calming effect. It's a good idea beforehand to request that your partner not respond to what you say while you are speaking. It works well if your partner listens attentively, lets love flow through his or her eyes, and occasionally comments, "I understand," or expresses how good it is that you are talking about this. An aura of trust, respect, and caring is essential.

Complete instructions and guidelines are given in Part Two of this book. They create ideal conditions for receiving maximum benefit from revealing your truth and listening to the truth of others.

CHAPTER THREE

HEARING
THE TRUTH

Two people we'll call "Janet" and "Michael," who had been
dating for about two years, were dining out one evening.
Michael saw a beautiful woman enter the restaurant, and his
look of admiration was plain to see. He said, "Janet, look at
that lovely woman. Doesn't she look a little like Brenda?"

Janet looked at the other woman, then fixed Michael with
an icy stare. "Don't you think it's rude of you to look at another
woman when you are out with me?"

The hurt in her eyes baffled Michael. How could such an
innocent remark affect her like this? In microseconds Michael
perceived a no-win situation for himself. How on earth was he
going to ignore the presence of half the human race just to keep

Janet feeling secure? He didn't think he could, and he really
didn't want to. Why couldn't they appreciate attractive
people together? Suddenly he felt angry and defiant.
"That's ridiculous!" he blurted. "I'm not being rude, and
I resent the accusation."

So there they were: two people in a romantic setting
who loved one another but feeling alienated by a wall of hurt
and fear, all because they attached meanings to one another's
comments that were inaccurate. When Michael referred to
the other woman as lovely, he wasn't saying she was more
beautiful than Janet, and he wasn't saying he'd like to have
sex with her—but that was what Janet heard. When Janet
said she thought it was rude for him to admire other women,
she wasn't saying what she truly meant. Her real message was,
"I feel hurt and unimportant to you when you admire other
women in front of me." Michael could have heard her
comment as a call for more acknowledgment and quieted
her fears with a simple statement such as, "There are many
beautiful women in the world, and you are more beautiful to
me than any of them. I regret my comment caused you pain.
I love you very much." But the primary force in his
communication was one of anger because he interpreted her
comment to mean he was going to have to choose between
being true to himself or suppressing himself to protect Janet
from her feelings of insecurity.

> If you make it
> difficult for
> people to be
> honest with
> you, most likely
> they won't be.

BECOMING A GOOD LISTENER

Are you the kind of person it is easy to be honest with? Or do people avoid you because you are judgmental or unkind or punishing? Many people gripe about others being dishonest with them, but rarely do they look at whether they are a safe person to be honest with. If you make it difficult for people to be honest with you, most likely they won't be. In this way you condemn yourself to a lifetime of superficial or adversarial relationships.

A good listener is someone who is curious, open-minded, and nonjudgmental. A good listener is not a know-it-all. A good listener knows that truth often reveals itself bit by bit, much like putting together a jigsaw puzzle. A good listener enjoys the process of discovery and doesn't jump to conclusions. A good listener doesn't interrupt, but lets people get it all out before responding. A good listener wants to know as much as possible before making an interpretation, if he or she chooses to make an interpretation at all. A good listener knows that the truth people start out with isn't necessarily the one they will wind up with when all the talking is done. A good listener has a talent for drawing out the truth from others in layers, helping people sort things through themselves and find their own solutions. A good listener gives people his or her full attention and asks for clarification when necessary. A good listener can tolerate

opinions different from his or her own without becoming
defensive or argumentative.

How you hear what someone says is determined by your
interpretations, and your interpretations flow from your past.
This is very important to know, especially if you find that you
overreact to what others say or habitually get your feelings hurt.
Our interpretations often come from misperceptions of other
people's meanings and intentions. We think they meant something
they didn't mean, and act as if what we thought they meant is
true when it isn't true at all. This happens frequently for most
people, probably including you. Remember, what someone said
is not necessarily what you heard, and what you heard is not
necessarily what they meant. This is why Clearing Processes—
a specific type of Heart-to-Heart Talk which we'll cover in detail
in Chapter Five—can have such magical and powerful effects.
They help you discover that the meaning you attached to
someone's conversation or action isn't necessarily the truth.

WHAT HAPPENS WHEN WE MISINTERPRET

For example, let's look at a couple who came to us for coaching
in their relationship. We'll call them "John" and "Sara." John
loved to play golf; it refreshed and revitalized him, and gave him

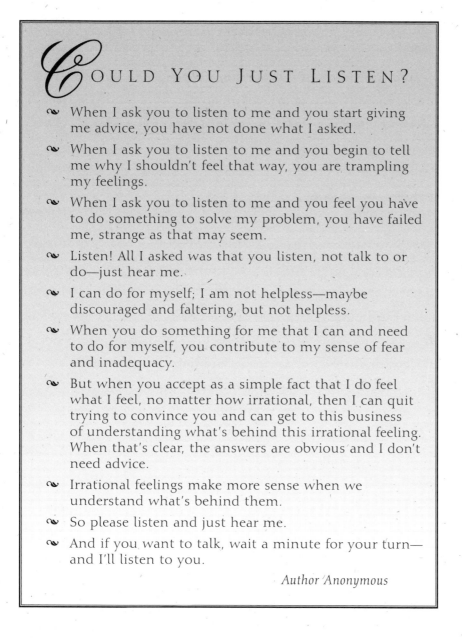

Could You Just Listen?

- When I ask you to listen to me and you start giving me advice, you have not done what I asked.

- When I ask you to listen to me and you begin to tell me why I shouldn't feel that way, you are trampling my feelings.

- When I ask you to listen to me and you feel you have to do something to solve my problem, you have failed me, strange as that may seem.

- Listen! All I asked was that you listen, not talk to or do—just hear me.

- I can do for myself; I am not helpless—maybe discouraged and faltering, but not helpless.

- When you do something for me that I can and need to do for myself, you contribute to my sense of fear and inadequacy.

- But when you accept as a simple fact that I do feel what I feel, no matter how irrational, then I can quit trying to convince you and can get to this business of understanding what's behind this irrational feeling. When that's clear, the answers are obvious and I don't need advice.

- Irrational feelings make more sense when we understand what's behind them.

- So please listen and just hear me.

- And if you want to talk, wait a minute for your turn—and I'll listen to you.

Author Anonymous

time to get things into a balanced perspective. Every once in
a while his grown daughter, Jenny, would call and ask to play
with him. When John called Sara one night to tell her he would
be playing golf with Jenny before dinner, Sara reacted by feeling
hurt and angry. The interpretations she placed on John's golf
game were that he enjoyed Jenny's company more than hers,
and that golf was more important to him than she was. (Note
that Sara didn't play golf.) She got so upset that she didn't even
hear that John was looking forward to their dinner that night.
If the two had never had a Heart-to-Heart Talk, Sara would still
be thinking that her interpretation was accurate and her feelings
of rejection were completely justified, and John would still be
baffled by her pain and upset. It was only after John listened
to her feelings and thoughts, and after she listened to his point
of view, that the situation got cleared up.

In another incident involving two couples, a much
anticipated holiday with some old friends almost turned into
a major disaster of hurt feelings and harsh words. "Dana" and
"Sam" hadn't seen "Laurel" and "Peter" for almost two years, as
they now lived in different states. Dana and Sam invited Laurel
and Peter to spend Christmas with them. It all began quite well,
but after a couple of days or so, Dana and Sam started feeling
irritated by their guests. They liked it when guests took care of
themselves and contributed to household responsibilities by
offering to share in daily chores.

Laurel and Peter were in a new environment, not knowing what was expected of them. They didn't know the standard modus operandi of the household or where things were kept. They had stayed with different friends all over the world and had been surprised on more than one occasion that, when they offered to share the expenses, their hosts got insulted and thought they were implying they were having a hard time with money. At other times, Laurel and Peter found that their offers to help tidy up were taken to mean that the hosts were sloppy. So this time, they decided to "go with the flow" and figured that if Dana or Sam wanted any specific help they would ask. However, Dana and Sam interpreted Laurel and Peter not bringing in firewood or volunteering to cook as an expectation to be waited upon.

The tension built in the household until Laurel and Peter started feeling unwelcome. Fortunately, they all knew they needed to have a talk. Once Dana and Sam understood Laurel and Peter's point of view, the situation was cleared up easily by making specific requests about what worked for them when having houseguests.

THE IMPORTANCE OF TAKING PERSONAL RESPONSIBILITY

If you want to be a safe person for others to be honest with, it is imperative that you learn to take responsibility for your own interpretations and the feelings that flow from them. The way you hear others' communication really says more about you than the person speaking. Truth is a gem of many facets. Each facet reflects the brilliance within and without. But the whole reveals a deeper, more profound message than all the parts by themselves. This is why it is so important for human beings to learn how to fit others' truths together with theirs and to perceive a greater harmonious whole, rather than battling over whose perception is "right" or more valuable and trying to control others into thinking exactly the same as they do. It may make people feel more secure when everyone agrees with them, but it won't create a world made rich by the unique and diverse expressions of the human soul. A world of monochromatic perceptions would soon become so boring that we would feel imprisoned by our security, and the splendor of what it is to be human would be lost to us. Without new and different ideas, we would cease to evolve as a species.

Observing the interpretations you place on other people's words and actions can reveal to you your own insecurities. This awareness gives you the clarity you need to grow stronger, which in turn allows you a higher tolerance for views other than your own. Listening to others and observing your reactions is one of the most accelerated growth and healing processes you can experience. It takes some know-how, and that is what the next chapter is about. Keep reading. This path holds the promise of love, wisdom, and strength beyond compare.

Truth is a gem of many facets.

CHAPTER FOUR

DEALING WITH
THE TRUTH

In dealing with the truth you have two basic options: reacting or responding. A *response* flows from mental clarity and emotional strength. It arises from the consideration of the long- and short-term consequences it would cause. A response is chosen to produce a desired outcome. A *reaction*, on the other hand, is an uncontrollable reflex born of fear. Its purpose is to defend against a perceived threat of danger or harm to yourself or those you care about. Reaction is a survival impulse. Yet fear is not always wise. Fear can cause you to act in ways wisdom would never consider. Fear would take you down the path of blame, while wisdom would lead you down the path of learning. The path of blame in human relationships leads you to unending recreations of the past. The path of learning leads you to healing and mastery.

In 1976, when we learned the difference between reacting and responding, it was an easy choice for us. We opted for the path of learning. We determined to overcome the fears that generated our reactions and to seek lessons from all our relationships with friend or foe. It has not always been easy, but it has always been rewarding. The path of learning is a marvelous adventure that would take many more books to explore in all its depth. Because we want you to be able to use communication processes right away and benefit from them immediately, we have purposely kept this book short. What follows are general guidelines to proceed down the path of learning and make sure your relationships are a place where honesty and love thrive.

How to Move From Reaction to Response

If you find that you have reacted to someone's speaking and would prefer to respond instead, you must first observe the way you heard what was said. What is the interpretation you have placed on the person's speaking? Are there any alternative interpretations available? Second, determine the speaker's intent. Is the person trying to hurt you, or simply revealing his or her thoughts and feelings? Don't rely on your own opinion; ask the person directly, "Why did you say that?" or "What is the purpose of your comment?" Of course, voice tone will have a major effect on whether your question is received as a question or as an attack. An inquisitive tone gives people the benefit of the doubt and works much better than a suspicious or accusatory tone.

Third, give yourself some time with your feelings before drawing conclusions or taking action. Refrain from arguing or trying to teach or persuade another when you are deeply upset. You want to honor your feelings in a safe and appropriate way that will bring you value. Emotion wisely expressed yields learning and healing, while emotion expressed for the purpose of hurting yields regret and guilt.

There is a big difference between acting out your feelings and honoring your feelings. Sometimes, as people learn to express their feelings, they go way overboard. They experience a huge pendulum swing from suppression to acting out. Just because you have a right to your feelings doesn't mean you are justified in blaming and attacking someone. You may feel hurt, but that doesn't mean the person tried to hurt you or is responsible for your pain. Your emotional reactions can often make the situation worse.

There is a big difference between acting out your feelings and honoring your feelings.

So, if you feel like lashing out, it is much better to express your feelings away from the person you want to blame. By handling intense feelings privately first, you avoid hurting anyone else, and you help yourself at the same time. It is more effective to sort things out with the other person after you have had an emotional release than to try and do it on top of your suppressed feelings. After the pain is released you will find yourself much more clear-headed and capable of making wise decisions.

If you feel yourself starting to "lose it" with someone, excuse yourself by saying something like, "I think it would be better for us to talk about this later. I want to sort through my feelings first." Then go to an appropriate place and let it out, with no holding back. Perhaps you need to have a good cry or let go of some anger. We don't want you to get the idea that you have to hide away your deep feelings—we simply caution you to be wise about the long-term effects on your relationships. Sometimes raw emotion comes out filled with blame, and blame damages relationships. If the relationship is healthy enough to tolerate the honest expression of deeply felt emotion, then expressing your feelings in the presence of another can be deeply healing. There are several ways of releasing anger so that no one gets hurt; find the way that works best for you.

Safe Ways to Release Anger

Some people find it helpful to write about their thoughts and feelings. To pour them all out onto a page without censoring or editing, then to reread them, can give you a new perspective. Other people need to see the physical effects of their anger. A feeling of satisfaction can come from breaking or tearing things. We have clients who go to thrift stores and buy old dishes and glasses to break, or clothes to rip apart, for whenever they need to vent their feelings. This way, later on, they won't have to lament the objects they destroyed.

Another great way to release anger is to have a "screaming pillow" into which you can holler at the top of your lungs; all anybody else can hear is a soft, muffled sound. We have designed screaming pillows for our clients to keep at home, in their cars, or at their office desks, and they work remarkably well. If you're a person who needs to whack things to release your anger, try punching bags. Or hitting old phone books with a 15-inch piece of hose can be very satisfying because of the wonderful thwacking sound it makes. Also, hitting the bed or kicking your heels while on the bed provides a good release. Find the ways that work for you, and have the necessary items ready for when you need them.

ARE YOU PROJECTING?

An important thing to observe about your reactions is to determine whether or not you are projecting. Webster defines projection as "the unconscious act of ascribing to another one's own undesirable ideas, impulses, or emotions, especially if they cause anxiety." Essentially, it means you judge in others what you are afraid to look at within yourself. Projection is an insidious tendency in humans. People feel so righteous when they are doing it, not even realizing they are projecting.

If you really want to overcome the fears that cause you to react, you must take control of your projections. But if it's an unconscious process, that's a pretty tall order, isn't it? How can you control something you don't even know you are doing? Luckily, there is a very big clue: Whenever you have a harsh judgment of another, you are projecting. In this context, judgment is different than discernment. Judgment condemns rather than simply observes. It's one thing to discern that someone is lying, and it's quite another to want to punish the person for it. If you have an overwhelming urge to punish someone, you are projecting. The person's words or actions have triggered your own self-doubt and unresolved fear from the past. The force of your fury is not driven by what is taking place in the present, but by something that happened in the past and which you are afraid will occur again in your future.

Do you remember what happened with Janet and Michael when he admired the beautiful woman in the restaurant? When Janet criticized Michael for being rude, she was projecting. Her fear (her undesirable impulse or emotion) was that she wasn't important or desirable enough to keep Michael's love. She was afraid she would lose him to a more beautiful woman. The anger in her statement to Michael didn't come from his comment; it came from her self-doubt.

So often people criticize their mates for being selfish and unloving. Even though sometimes there may be an element of truth, the torrent of pain they feel comes from the deep hidden belief or fear that they are unlovable and don't deserve the kind of love they want. They are projecting their undesirable emotions onto their mate and blaming their mate for it—often when their mate really does love them.

We have one client, "Beth," who was enjoying the best relationship with a man she had ever had. His name was "David." Beth's problem was that she just couldn't get over the judgments she was having about David, and it was starting to affect their sex life. David, a man in his early fifties, had taken two years off to reassess his life. He had started working with his father's company in his late teens and had worked there all his life. His lack of passion for this became too painful, and he

Whenever you have a harsh judgment of another, you are projecting.

decided to take some time to rediscover himself. He wanted to make sure the rest of his life was going to please him rather than please his father. It was a brave thing to do, and quite uncomfortable at times, since he sometimes confused his worth as a person with the notion of being a hard-working, productive man valued for what he did rather than who he was.

David was quite handsome, sophisticated, loving, and tender. He was Beth's ideal mate in all ways except for his lack of career. Beth loved David, but when she discovered that he had been living off his savings for the last two years, something just "clicked" in her. She shut down sexually, much to her surprise and disappointment. Suddenly she started feeling critical of David. She looked for ways in which he was inadequate and incompetent, and she began snapping at him over small things. He became increasingly dissatisfied with the relationship. Neither of them understood what had happened.

Clearly, Beth had started projecting on David. Even though she was a career woman with a determined drive to achieve, she had a hidden, *unconscious* fear that she couldn't take care of herself and needed someone to take care of her. She thought she needed a wealthy, financially independent man to save her when she needed it. When she heard David had only one more year's worth of savings to live on, she unknowingly interpreted that to mean David couldn't be there for her when she needed him and that she couldn't trust him anymore.

If you find that you are projecting, be honest about it, then apologize.

When Beth discovered she had done this, she was embarrassed. She didn't resist the awareness of her projection, for this realization had the ring of truth as the source of the whole problem. This realization also brought with it a different strategy for solution. If she wanted her relationship with David to mature in love and harmony, the task at hand was to resolve the fears of poverty that were born of her childhood and resulted in her projection. She needed to take back control from her "projecting mind" and see the truth: David was a capable, strong, wise man who had the good sense to take control of his own life and make sure it was what he wanted it to be. The truth also was that Beth was a vital, creative woman who could depend on her own strength. The notion that she needed a man to take care of her financially was not grounded in the facts.

Beth took charge of her projecting, judgmental mind. She stopped snapping at David and criticizing him. As soon as she started trusting him more, her sex drive returned. Today they are both very much in love and are planning a future together.

If you find that you are projecting, be honest about it. Tell the other person, "I reacted so strongly because what you said brought up my (fears, judgments, etc.) about myself, and I feel upset when that happens." Then apologize sincerely, and make it clear that your reaction was really about something that happened in your past rather than about what the person said or did.

WHAT IS YOUR DESIRED OUTCOME?

When others can be honest with you, you will have more love, trust, understanding, and intimacy.

When the other person speaks his or her truth, consider what is the most beneficial response. Remember, a *response* is chosen to produce a desired outcome, so think about what this is. Is it to reestablish harmony or work together to create a mutually beneficial result? If it is to punish, blame, or make the other person wrong, you'll have to read another book. *Straight From the Heart* was written to help people who care about one another, want to feel more connected, and are building more trust and understanding in their relationship. Blame, punishment, and making others wrong generate adversarial relationships where love withers and eventually dies.

After you know your desired outcome, look for the best way to bring it about. Is it a conversation with the other person to discuss feelings and/or solutions? Is an apology appropriate? Is it bringing in a third party to facilitate clarity, understanding, or healing?

Remember, responding to others' communication makes you a safe person to be honest with. When others can be honest with you, you will have more love, trust, understanding, and intimacy in your life. You may need to grow to overcome your tendency to react, but the emotional strength you receive will bring you strong, loving, trustworthy, and lasting relationships.

You now have the basics to step through love's doorway. We offer our best wishes for this, your great adventure of the heart.

Part Two

STEPPING THROUGH THE OPEN DOOR

Why do we not hear the truth?

Because we do not speak it.

PUBLILIUS SYRUS

CHAPTER FIVE
HOW TO HAVE
HEART-TO-HEART TALKS

Language and communication are fundamental to human beings and to relationships. Language and communication are to us as water is to fish or the air is to birds. Fish are biologically structured to function in water. Birds are biologically structured to function in the air. In the same way, language is a part of our biological structure, integral to who we are and how we experience our reality. Most of the time we speak, listen, and communicate without thinking. It's automatic, just as fish swim and birds fly. Yet the possibilities for our relationships, being socially constructed through language, are opened or closed by what we say and hear, and how we speak and listen.

Heart-to-Heart Talks are structured in a particular way that may seem artificial and contrived because they require you to speak and listen in a way that is different than how you are accustomed. They may feel strange or unusual in the beginning. That's okay, it's normal—practically everybody encounters this. After awhile, when you have experienced the enormous value of using these processes, they won't seem so strange. In fact, you will come to cherish them and what they do for you and your relationships.

These communication processes are deceptively simple. Just glancing through each of the following chapters doesn't reveal the powerful positive impact they will have on your relationships, just as looking at an acorn cannot show you the splendor of the mighty oak contained within. These communication processes are seeds that with proper planting will yield you the fruits of understanding, compassion, patience, love, trust, intimacy, self-acceptance, healing, mutual empowerment, and peace.

Heart-to-Heart Talks are carefully designed to meet specific purposes. When used as recommended, these processes retrain you so that you don't fall into the "normal" conversation habits that generate so much frustration and estrangement. For example, have you ever been talking to people and felt as though they aren't really listening to you? They may be looking at you, but their attention seems to be elsewhere—perhaps already preparing what they are going to say in response to your speaking, or being distracted by something else. Most people need to be retrained to really listen to someone.

Another example is when you are talking to people and your words spark a memory or emotion about something in their own life, and they jump in excitedly to talk about themselves. It leaves you feeling unheard and unimportant, doesn't it? Perhaps you do this with others, making them feel the same way. Or perhaps if people are telling you about a problem they are having with you, you don't even let them finish—you interrupt them to defend yourself. This behavior is a handicap in any relationship, for it makes people reluctant to bring up issues that can only be resolved by open sharing and mutual problem solving.

WHAT YOU CAN EXPECT

The beauty of Heart-to-Heart Talks is that they provide structure for your communication. Structure is to these processes what soil is to a seed. The soil provides a foundation, a place for the roots to take hold. The roots give nourishment to the young tree as well as the stability and strength it needs to grow to its full size. The structure of these communication processes creates a foundation of safety, respect, tolerance, and clarity that can support you through difficult times and help your relationships achieve their full potential.

Of course, other things are needed to nurture a seed into a sapling, then into a mighty oak. For openers, your personal truth is like water to the seed. Just as water germinates the seed, your truth sparks new growth in your relationships; without a constant supply of it, they will wither away. Another essential ingredient to bring to your relationships is love. Love is like the warmth of the sun, bringing sustenance, healing, and comfort to a cold, hardened heart. Without the life-giving force of the sun, none of us on this planet could exist. The same is true of love. Some people have lived so long feeling isolated and misunderstood that their hearts are heavily guarded lest they be hurt anymore. Your focused love during a Heart-to-Heart Talk can help people to gently open just as a flower opens to the sun. Only when people's hearts are open can they feel connected with others. This feeling of connection will grow into more love, trust, understanding, and intimacy in your relationships with them.

Heart-to-Heart Talks heal and strengthen your inner self. Just as a plant flourishes in a greenhouse, these processes furnish an environment for your relationships to flourish. They help you discover more of yourself, to know with greater clarity than ever before who you are and what you need so you can be more completely yourself with others. With these processes you become like a full-grown tree with strong roots to support you,

Your truth sparks new growth in your relationships.

outreaching branches to receive the fullness of the sun's light, and the strength and stature to offer shade and comfort to the weary at heart. You have the power and skill to create relationships filled with love, peace, encouragement, and expanding possibilities.

DIFFERENT PROCESSES FOR DIFFERENT PURPOSES

There are four kinds of processes that make up Heart-to-Heart Talks:

1. Nurturing Processes
2. Clearing Processes
3. Discovery Processes
3. Affirming Processes

Nurturing Processes do exactly what they say: nurture the relationship and make it stronger. They generate mental and emotional well-being. They bring healing, nurturing energy to the relationship so that it can flourish, just as sunlight, water, and fertilizer bring healing, nurturing energy to a garden. Without these elements, any garden will soon wither and die. It is the same with relationships: If nurturing elements are not brought to a relationship on a regular basis, it, too, will soon waste away.

Clearing Processes allow you to talk about your fears, anxieties, and concerns in a way that allows you to let go of them—to clear them—so that you can see new possibilities and opportunities that are difficult or impossible to see when your vision is clouded by emotion and fear. Just as all gardens grow weeds that need to be cleared out, all relationships require careful maintenance. These processes are like the weeding activities in a garden.

Clearing Processes are very powerful and can be used effectively to release fears, reduce stress, and increase intimacy. One of the long-term effects of withholding communication is that people cannot feel the love others have for them. They are so filled with thoughts and feelings of hurt, disappointment, resentment, or suspicion that they have no room for anything else. Love bounces off them like bullets off Superman's chest. But after you complete a Clearing Process, you will notice a much deeper feeling of connection results from your Nurturing and Affirming Processes.

Discovery Processes promote understanding. They enable you to learn more about yourself and your partner, and your partner about you. Sometimes we don't know what we really think about something until we talk about it out loud. That's what Discovery Processes help you do in a structured and predictable way.

Affirming Processes build affinity with others. As you support one another in strengthening self-esteem and self-respect, you will develop the kinds of qualities to which you both aspire. These processes will result in strong alliances with your friends and loved ones so that your relationships feel like an oasis of encouragement and expanding possibilities.

It's best in using these processes to start small and work your way up. To begin, we recommend you select three different processes in any of the following sequences:

Nurturing ∾ Clearing ∾ Affirming

Affirming ∾ Clearing ∾ Nurturing

Nurturing ∾ Discovery ∾ Affirming

Affirming ∾ Discovery ∾ Nurturing

It's important to sandwich Clearing and Discovery Processes in between Nurturing and Affirming Processes. In any event, *never do a Clearing Process without following it up with a Nurturing or Affirming Process.*

As you become more adept in your Heart-to-Heart Talks, you may do as many processes as you want in one sitting. Regardless of how many processes you use, always start—and finish—with a Nurturing or an Affirming Process.

How to Initiate a Heart-to-Heart Talk

There are many ways to get someone to do these processes with you. What we recommend is the straightforward method. Approach the person in the spirit of respect, cooperation, and a mutual desire to improve your communication skills and/or relationship. If the person also values these things, or is at least open to learning, then there is less chance of argument or resistance. We've found that most people are aware that they need at least a little improvement in the area of communication and, in fact, many of them will probably be glad or even relieved if you bring it up.

Here are some conversation openers that have worked for people we know:

"I care a lot about our relationship, and I wonder if you'd be willing to do a process with me that I just found out about. I think it could really open up the channels of communication and make it easier for us to say the things we need to say."

"I feel really good about us right now, and I'm looking for ways to make it even better. Would you be able to help me out?"

"Since we're all interested in making this task force more efficient, I'd like to propose a communication process that I think can take our degree of teamwork to a new level. Would you like to hear about it?"

"I feel like we've been walking on eggshells around each other lately, and I'm ready to try something different. I just learned about a process called a Heart-to-Heart Talk that I'd love to try with you. It takes only a few minutes, and it would mean a lot if you could play along with me."

"Have you been feeling the same thing I've been feeling lately? Like we really need to clear the air? I have an idea I think could help."

Another possibility is to show your friend a copy of this book, and invite him or her to review the checklist in the front. ("Do I deflect praise and compliments by downplaying them?" "Do I avoid necessary confrontations?") Chances are good that at least a few of these points will hit home. Be there with your friend to discuss these ideas further, or follow up a couple of days later to see if you can answer any questions.

Of course, nothing works as well as doing the process itself. Nurturing Processes are especially good introductions to Heart-to-Heart Talks, as they instantly create a safe place for your communication and allow both of you to give and receive simultaneously. Reassure your friend that it's natural to feel unsure or awkward at first, and make it clear that the purpose of the exercise isn't to orchestrate a certain result or to analyze what was said. The purpose of a Nurturing Process is to nurture, the purpose of a Clearing Process is to clear, and so on. Simply let the truth and the love flow, and your rewards will be great.

Nothing works as well as doing the process itself.

Guidelines for Heart-to-Heart Talks

In all our communication processes, we followed these basic guidelines. They are a major component in the success of any Heart-to-Heart Talk. We strongly recommend you read them aloud with your partner at the beginning of each session for the first several sessions until you feel you remember them very well, then review them periodically as a refresher.

GUIDELINES

1. We will communicate with the intention of producing more harmony and understanding.

2. We are committed to a positive outcome for both of us.

3. We acknowledge we are responsible for our own feelings.

4. We are open to giving and receiving support from one another.

5. We will do our best to hold in mind the "highest spiritual truth" about each other as we communicate our fears and upsets.

6. We are willing to speak the whole truth about our thoughts and feelings.

7. We will do our best to face our fears rather than avoid them.

8. We will practice forgiveness with ourselves and one another, recognizing that mistakes call for correction, not judgment or punishment.

9. We will continue to communicate even if an upset arises.

10. We will use upsets to learn about ourselves and use the situation to become wiser, more lovable and loving people.

11. We will breathe deeply in order to remain in touch with our feelings.

12. We will respect one another's confidences and not discuss the substance of our communication unless we both agree otherwise.

THE FORMAT OF HEART-TO-HEART TALKS

NURTURING, CLEARING, DISCOVERY, AND AFFIRMING PROCESSES

1. Set aside a quiet place to do this process, where you and your partner will not be disturbed for at least 20 minutes.

2. Sit across from your partner, facing each other at a comfortable distance (about 2–3 feet) so that your knees are almost touching.

3. Decide beforehand which one of you will go first. Both of you should state your intention(s) and review the Guidelines for Heart-to-Heart Talks on page 59.

4. To do the process, the first partner has two minutes in which to complete the statement as many times as he or she can, while the second partner listens. (See the example following these instructions, in which the first partner is "A" and the second partner is "B.")

5. When A's turn is up, B completes the same statement as many times as possible in the two-minute period.

6. If you have any anxiety at all about doing these processes, it is extremely valuable to begin with a specific Clearing Process to make it easier to proceed. Say, "A fear (concern, reservation) I have about doing these processes is...". (See the example on page 63.) This will allow you both to clear anything that may be in the way of participating fully and receiving the value of Heart-to-Heart Talks.

7. As you are speaking, there may be times when nothing comes immediately to mind. *It is important to keep your momentum going, so simply say "blank," then continue immediately with the next statement.* ("Something I feel good about is knowing you'll pick me up tomorrow," "Something I feel good about is—*blank*,"

"Something I feel good about is the trip to the mountains my fiancee and I are planning....") By following this structure rather than pausing and searching for something to say, you allow yourself to access a deeper level of mind and heart.

8. It is important to breathe as fully and deeply as you can while you are doing these processes. Often when people do something unfamiliar, they have a tendency to become stiff and tense, breathing shallowly or even holding their breath. Heart-to-Heart Talks work best when you are both in a relaxed, receptive state. Breathe slowly and deeply. Imagine the tension sinking from your body into the floor, and feel your partner's love and acceptance pour in even as you give it in return.

9. Affirming Processes are slightly different and a little more free form than the other processes. A begins by making an affirming statement about B, and B responds receptively. A then repeats the same statement, or a variation, to B, and the process continues in this way with both partners building energy in their voices and bodies until A's turn is up, and the excitement is positively outrageous. (See the example on page 73.) Then they switch.

10. As you are learning to do these processes, it is a good idea to set a timer so you will know when each partner's turn is complete. As you become more experienced, you will develop greater trust in your own feelings and a surer sense of whether or not you have said all you need to say. At that point, you and your partner can each take more than one turn for a particular process if necessary.

11. At the conclusion of the Heart-to-Heart Talk, hug your partner.

12. *Important:* In doing these processes, you may find that you want—or need—to have detailed conversations about topics that arise. *While Heart-to-Heart Talks are ideal for identifying these areas, they are not the place to do this.* Wait until after you have concluded your Heart-to-Heart Talk to have conversations specifically for seeking solutions: trouble shooting, brainstorming, negotiating issues, and so on.

WHEN YOU ARE THE SPEAKER

1. Say the first thing that comes to your mind.

2. Do not censor yourself, or say what you think the other person "wants" to hear, or worry that the other person will think less of you.

3. Speak your truth at all times. Allow all your thoughts and feelings to come up without judgment. Powerful emotions may be stirred up—don't be concerned; just let them surface.

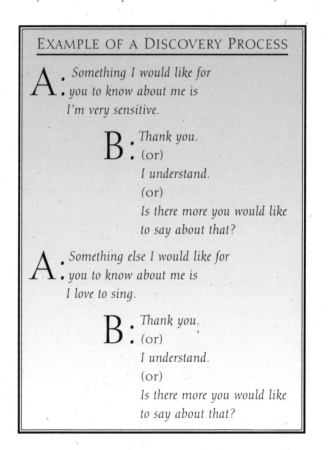

EXAMPLE OF A DISCOVERY PROCESS

A: *Something I would like for you to know about me is I'm very sensitive.*

B: *Thank you.*
(or)
I understand.
(or)
Is there more you would like to say about that?

A: *Something else I would like for you to know about me is I love to sing.*

B: *Thank you.*
(or)
I understand.
(or)
Is there more you would like to say about that?

WHEN YOU ARE THE LISTENER

1. For the next two minutes, your partner is the focus of your universe. Listen with every ounce of your being—your face, your eyes, the way you hold your body.

2. As your partner is speaking, resist the temptation to try to "fix" what you may perceive to be the person's problem. Do not try to give advice or offer judgments, opinions, or analyses. Simply give your partner your full attention.

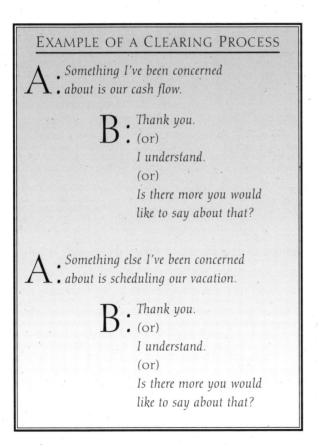

EXAMPLE OF A CLEARING PROCESS

A: *Something I've been concerned about is our cash flow.*

B: *Thank you.*
(or)
I understand.
(or)
Is there more you would like to say about that?

A: *Something else I've been concerned about is scheduling our vacation.*

B: *Thank you.*
(or)
I understand.
(or)
Is there more you would like to say about that?

STAY IN THE STRUCTURE
UNTIL YOU'RE COMPLETE

It is important to understand why the listener says, "Thank you" or "I understand." "Thank you" is short for "Thank you for telling me that." "I understand" is short for "I understand what you are saying to me." Neither response means agreement or disagreement, or that anyone is right or wrong, simply that you have heard your partner and witnessed his or her personal reality at the moment. If you do not understand what has been said, you may say "I didn't understand what you said, can you please say it in a different way?" This is similar to "Is there more you would like to say about that?"

When you are getting emotional in Heart-to-Heart Talks there is a very strong tendency to want to get into a conversation or a debate about what your partner has said. You will be able to feel this tendency as a physical sensation in your body. If you give in to that urge and break the structure of the Heart-to-Heart Talk, the process will disintegrate and will no longer work for you. It is imperative that you stay within the structure of Heart-to-Heart Talks until the process is complete. Once everyone has said what they need to say and heard what needs to be heard within the structure, then you may enter into conversation for solution, change, or whatever needs to happen.

USE HEART-TO-HEART TALKS TO HEAL, NOT TO HURT

These communication processes are powerful tools to facilitate emotional release and healing. They allow you to open up, connect with people in your life, and feel more love, joy, trust, and understanding. They give you an opportunity to nurture yourself and others, to create a safe place for growth and exploration. Above all, *their purpose is to honor your relationships.* This is why it is so important always to include nurturing in whatever you do. So whenever you do a Clearing Process, follow it with a Nurturing Process. Without this essential step, a Heart-to-Heart Talk would be incomplete—like putting your right leg into a pair of pants, but not your left leg. Adhere to the following dos and don'ts for ensuring that your Heart-to-Heart Talks foster growth, respect, and healing.

DON'T

- ᦥ Don't use Clearing Processes, or any other process, to hurt your partner.

- ᦥ Don't use offensive language or call the other person names.

- ᦥ Don't speak in "you" sentences that cast blame or denigrate a person's character. ("Something that irritates me is how self-righteous you are.")

- ᦥ Don't speak in generalities or exaggerations. ("Something that irritates me is how you always interrupt whenever anyone else is trying to talk." "Something that concerns me is that you ignore me constantly.")

- ᦥ Don't use a Clearing Process without following it up with a Nurturing or Affirming Process.

DO

- ᦥ Speak in "I" sentences. ("Something I need to say is that I got really scared and upset when you and your brother were yelling at each other on the phone last night.")

- ᦥ Speak as specifically as possible. ("Something I've been afraid to tell you is that I feel unimportant when we eat dinner and you read the newspaper instead of talking with me.")

- ᦥ Apologize to the other person when this is called for. ("Something I need to say is that I projected my anger on to you in the meeting last week, and I apologize. That's not anything I would want to do again.")

- ᦥ Follow a Clearing Process with a Nurturing or Affirming Process.

- ᦥ Turn complaints into specific requests. ("Something that irritates me is when I see wet towels left on the bedroom carpet, and it would really help me if you could hang them on the towel rack instead.")

THE MENU OF PROCESSES

The next nine chapters contain communication processes you can use as the basis of your Heart-to-Heart Talks in these areas:

1. Building Friendship
2. Discovering the Self
   - ✺ Strengths
   - ✺ Spirituality
   - ✺ Dreams and Visions
   - ✺ Fears
   - ✺ Guilt
   - ✺ Resentment
   - ✺ Withholding
3. Forgiveness and Healing Hurts
4. Deepening Intimacy and Trust
5. Bonding with Family
6. Enhancing Ties with Co-Workers
7. Creating Love and Romance
8. Sharing Power and Co-Creation
9. Windows of the Soul

CHAPTER SIX

BUILDING
FRIENDSHIP

Do you have a true-blue, loyal friend? Someone you know
would always stand by your side no matter what happened?
For some people this is a childhood buddy, someone who has
shared the joys and pains of growing up. For others this is their
mate, or their brother or sister, or a friend they met later in
life—someone who accepts them exactly as they are.

   Would you like to enjoy that same sense of connection
with other people? Perhaps someone with whom you already
feel close, but you'd like to feel even closer? Ask this person if
he or she would be willing to take a few minutes to participate
in a Heart-to-Heart Talk with you. Explain that this process
creates a safe place in which to open up and express what's

really on your mind and in your heart. The benefits will be felt immediately. Be sure to include lots of Nurturing Processes, as these are just as essential to the growth of a healthy relationship as sun, water, and soil are to a garden.

NURTURING PROCESSES

Something I like about you is...

Something I respect about you is...

Something I admire about you is...

Something I love about you is...

Something I feel good about is...

One of the happiest times I have had with you is...

One of the ways I like to express my love is...

One of the ways I like to be loved is...

Something I would like to experience more with you is...

Something I would like to be acknowledged for is...

Something I would like to acknowledge you for is...

Something I like about myself is...

Something I am thankful for is...

Something I love in my life is...

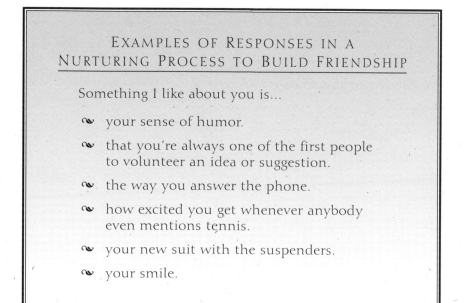

EXAMPLES OF RESPONSES IN A
NURTURING PROCESS TO BUILD FRIENDSHIP

Something I like about you is...

∾ your sense of humor.

∾ that you're always one of the first people
to volunteer an idea or suggestion.

∾ the way you answer the phone.

∾ how excited you get whenever anybody
even mentions tennis.

∾ your new suit with the suspenders.

∾ your smile.

CLEARING PROCESSES

Something I am concerned about is...

Something I need to say is...

Something I think you should know is...

Something I have been afraid to tell you is...

Something that irritates me is...

A feeling I have been having is...

One of my fears about doing these processes is...

One of my fears about continuing these processes is...

DISCOVERY PROCESSES

Something I would like for you to know about me is...

Something I have always wanted is...

Something I want in my relationships is...

Something that's difficult for me in relationships is...

Something I would like to change or improve in my relationships is...

Something that is important to me in relationships is...

Something I'm interested in is...

Something I don't want in my relationships is...

Something I am afraid of in relationships is...

AFFIRMING PROCESSES

It's good for you to ask for what you want.

You are a beautiful, lovable person, and you deserve to be loved!

Your presence alone is a contribution to others.

You are a person of great love, wisdom, and power.

You deserve to be acknowledged and appreciated.

Please feel free to make up your own.

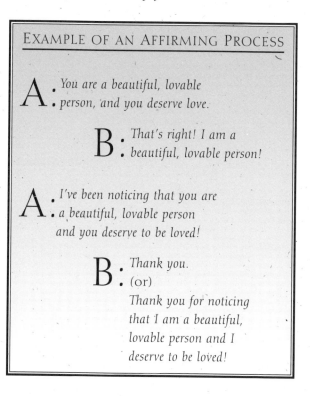

EXAMPLE OF AN AFFIRMING PROCESS

A: *You are a beautiful, lovable person, and you deserve love.*

B: *That's right! I am a beautiful, lovable person!*

A: *I've been noticing that you are a beautiful, lovable person and you deserve to be loved!*

B: *Thank you.*
(or)
Thank you for noticing that I am a beautiful, lovable person and I deserve to be loved!

CHAPTER SEVEN

DISCOVERING
THE SELF

Discovering yourself and another can be a journey of adventure
and healing. We as human beings are very much the same
in some ways and very different in others. Often we make
assumptions about others without even knowing it. These
processes can help you to understand one another better,
to appreciate the differences and find joy in the similarities.
Generally speaking, most people are not self-reflective enough.
They act out of unexamined beliefs and attitudes that may
not serve them in the best ways possible. When you do these
processes you may find yourself saying things that surprise you.
Your self-knowledge will grow by leaps and bounds, giving
you the power to change what you want to change and to be

thankful for the *you* that you have become already. They are designed to help you focus on several specific areas:

- ∾ Strengths
- ∾ Spirituality
- ∾ Dreams and Visions
- ∾ Fears
- ∾ Guilt
- ∾ Resentment
- ∾ Withholding

As you and your partner embark on these processes, release the need to edit or analyze. Speak your uncensored truths as freely as possible. Just as with the other exercises in this book— and particularly with these—the first things you tend to say will be closer to your level of conscious awareness, but the longer you continue, the deeper you will go.

In reviewing and selecting these processes, you will find they are organized by subject area. For the purposes of this chapter, all of these processes (except the Affirming Processes) can be considered Discovery Processes. Approach them in a spirit of adventure, and prepare for powerful revelations.

STRENGTHS

Something I am good at is...

Something that makes me happy is...

Something that is important to me is...

One of the things I like best about myself is...

People can count on me to...

SPIRITUALITY

Spirituality is important because...

Something that confuses me about spirituality is...

I resist spiritual things because...

Something I believe about God/a Higher Power is...

If I were more spiritual I would...

DREAMS AND VISIONS

Something I have always wanted to do is...

Something I could contribute to others is...

I am afraid I cannot achieve my goals because...

Something that needs to happen for me to achieve my goals is...

It is important to have goals because...

It is important to "think big" because...

Something I would do if I could not fail is...

If I could do anything I would...

EXAMPLES OF RESPONSES
IN A PROCESS TO DISCOVER THE SELF

If I could do anything I would...

- ∾ take that trip to Greece.
- ∾ say what's really on my mind and not be afraid to speak up anymore.
- ∾ eat dessert every night!
- ∾ fly, free as a bird.
- ∾ go into the teaching profession.
- ∾ enjoy sunsets (or sunrises!) with my lover as often as possible.
- ∾ invent a way to clean up the oceans.
- ∾ laugh or cry whenever I felt like it.

FEARS

Something I am concerned about is...

Something I need to say is...

Something I have been afraid to tell you is...

Something I am afraid of in life (relationships, work, etc.) is...

One of the things I hate about fear is...

Something I get out of being afraid is...

I am afraid because...

Something that would help me release my fear is...

One of the ways I play it safe is...

Something I feel apprehensive about is...

If I were not afraid of _____ I would...

If I were not afraid I would...

Something I have always wanted but have been afraid to ask for is...

One of my fears about doing these processes is...

One of my fears about continuing these processes is...

GUILT

Something I feel guilty about is...

One of the ways I deprive myself is...

One of the ways I punish myself is...

Guilt makes me...

Something that would help me release my guilt is...

If I did not feel guilty I would...

Through the power of Divine Love I now forgive myself for...

Through the power of Divine Love I now forgive others
(my father, my mother, etc.) for...

RESENTMENT

Something I feel resentful about is...

If I were not resentful I would...

Resentment keeps me from...

Something I get out of being resentful is...

Something that would help me let go of resentment is...

Others' resentment makes me...

WITHHOLDING

Something I am afraid to say is...

I would not want people to see that I am...

One of the reasons I do not speak my mind is...

One of the ways I hold myself back is...

One of the ways I withhold my love is...

One of the ways I isolate myself is...

One of the reasons I withhold is...

The benefits I receive from withholding are...

It's not safe to love because...

It's not safe to tell the truth because...

AFFIRMING PROCESSES

You are Divinely protected on your path of healing.

You have everything it takes to succeed in life.

You are a powerful magnet for all the good that you deserve.

You deserve to be loved and appreciated by people.

It is safe and rewarding for you to express your true thoughts and feelings with others.

The beauty of your Spirit shines brightly as you release your fears.

Please feel free to make up your own.

CHAPTER EIGHT

FORGIVENESS
AND HEALING HURTS

When was the last time you allowed yourself to cry out of sadness or loss or anger or disappointment? Somewhere in the journey to adulthood, we were taught that it was unacceptable to reveal our true thoughts and feelings, especially the "bad" ones. We learned to bury our emotions and pretend they didn't exist, and we started to build walls so that the people we cared about most wouldn't discover how "unworthy" we were.

The first step on the path to healing is to learn to recognize and acknowledge your true feelings. Just as a poisonous weed choking the growth of a garden, your suppressed resentment, anger, and fear must be dug up to be eliminated. It may seem intimidating at first to consider doing these processes with

someone you know well, such as a friend or family member.
But as you both state your intentions and commit to your
mutual growth, this will only strengthen the bond between you.
Begin and end with lots of Nurturing and Affirming Processes.
Trust in the healing power of love.

NURTURING PROCESSES

I am now willing to forgive _____ for...

I am now willing to forgive myself for...

Through the power of Divine Love I now
forgive _____ for...

Something I like about you is...

Something I respect about you is...

Something I admire about you is...

Something I love about you is...

One of the happiest times I have had with you is...

One of the ways I like to be loved is...

One of the ways I like to express my love is...

Something I would like to be acknowledged for is...

Something I would like to acknowledge you for is...

Something I like about myself is...

Something I would like to experience more with you is...

Something I am thankful for is...

Something I love in my life is...

CLEARING PROCESSES

Something I am concerned about is...

Something I need to say is...

Something that irritates me is...

Something I think you should know is...

A feeling I have been having is...

Something I have been afraid to tell you is...

One of my fears about doing these processes is...

One of my fears about continuing these processes is...

EXAMPLES OF RESPONSES IN A
CLEARING PROCESS TO FORGIVE AND HEAL HURTS

Something I need to say is...

- ❧ I don't like it when you argue with your dad and then won't talk to me afterward.

- ❧ I feel jealous sometimes.

- ❧ When you tell me how to do things a certain way, I feel criticized.

- ❧ It really hurt my feelings when you made that comment about my friend the other day.

- ❧ I can't stand the color yellow!

- ❧ You don't have to impress me in order for me to love you.

DISCOVERY PROCESSES

Something I would like you to know about me is...

Something I have always wanted is...

Something I want in my relationships is...

Something that's difficult for me in relationships is...

Something I think you should know is...

Something I feel hurt about is...

A hurt I have been carrying for a long time is...

Someone who is hard for me to forgive is...

Something I blame myself for is...

Forgiveness is important because...

Something I don't want in my relationships is...

Something I am afraid of in relationships is...

AFFIRMING PROCESSES

It is safe and rewarding for you to feel your true feelings.

The more you heal the past, the happier and stronger you feel.

You deserve to be loved and forgiven.

You have everything it takes to heal and forgive the past.

A wonderful world of peace and acceptance is opening up for you.

The healing power of love and wisdom is moving throughout your life.

Please feel free to make up your own.

CHAPTER NINE

DEEPENING
INTIMACY AND TRUST

Having trust and intimacy in our relationships is essential to our well-being. Because we are social animals, we need to feel connected to other people. Someone who goes about day-to-day business without trusting anybody is only half-alive and is missing out on life's greatest rewards. Does this sound like you or someone you know?

The Heart-to-Heart Talks in this chapter are an ideal way to release fears and let in the healing power of love. As you do these processes, you'll find that the more trust you place in others, the more you will enjoy from them in return, and the more comfortable you will feel receiving their trust. That's because these processes are carefully structured to be nonjudgmental and nonthreatening. Do them on a consistent basis, and it will take your communication skills, sensitivity, and emotional capacity to much higher levels than you ever dreamed possible.

NURTURING PROCESSES

One of the reasons I am trustworthy is...

One of the ways I like to express my love is...

One of the ways I like to be loved is...

Something I would like to be acknowledged for is...

Something I would like to acknowledge you for is...

Something I like about myself is...

Something I like about you is...

Something I respect about you is...

Something I admire about you is...

Something I love about you is...

Something I am thankful for is...

Something I love in my life is...

Something I feel good about is...

Something I would like to experience more with you is...

CLEARING PROCESSES

Something I am concerned about is...

Something I need to say is...

Something that irritates me is...

Something I think you should know is...

A feeling I have been having is...

Something I have been afraid to tell you is...

One of my fears about doing these processes is...

One of my fears about continuing these processes is....

DISCOVERY PROCESSES

One of the ways I know I can trust someone is...

Something that scares me about intimacy is...

Trusting others is difficult for me because...

What happens for me when I stop trusting is...

One of the ways I avoid intimacy is...

Something I think you should know is...

Trusting others is easy for me because...

One of the ways I could be more trustworthy is...

Something I would like for you to know about me is...

Something I have always wanted is...

Something I want in my relationships is...

Something that's difficult for me in relationships is...

Something I would like to change or improve in my relationships is...

Something I don't want in my relationships is...

Something I am afraid of in relationships is...

One of the reasons intimacy is important is...

EXAMPLES OF RESPONSES
IN A DISCOVERY PROCESS
TO DEEPEN INTIMACY AND TRUST

One of the ways I avoid intimacy is...

∾ by shutting down.

∾ letting myself get stressed out, then snapping
   at people.

∾ watching TV every night after dinner.

∾ having to be strong all the time.

∾ not admitting to you how I really feel.

∾ burying my nose in a book.

AFFIRMING PROCESSES

It is safe and rewarding to trust others.

It is safe and rewarding for you to be open and vulnerable.

The more people get to know you, the more they like you.

People want you to be happy and to have what you want.

People accept and appreciate you just the way you are.

People deserve to receive your love.

Please feel free to make up your own.

CHAPTER TEN

BONDING

WITH FAMILY

Our relationships with our parents, children, siblings, and extended family members can be the greatest source of life's richest emotions—joy, nurturing, intimacy, trust, unconditional love. Without ongoing and conscious nurturing, however, your ties with the people closest to you will suffer. Also, because there is so much "history" with the people you grew up with, it's especially crucial to use Clearing Processes to dispel what may be years of buried resentments, disappointment, and guilt.

Take heart in the fact that these processes can be the greatest gift of healing you could give to the people you love. They are especially powerful when used in combination with processes from "Forgiveness and Healing Hurts" and/or "Deepening Intimacy and Trust."

For the Heart-to-Heart Talks in this chapter, a group format can be used in addition to the usual one-on-one format. Hold a "family council" in which everyone sits close together in a circle, and go around systematically until everyone has had a turn. Whoever is speaking gets to hold a special object which has been selected beforehand—an interesting stone or piece of quartz, an acorn, a heart-shaped beanbag, a beautiful feather, a carved stick—to signify that this person has the floor. Only the person holding this object may speak. When this person's turn is over, the special object is passed to the next speaker.

For simplicity's sake the listeners, rather than responding verbally, should merely nod to signify that they understand what the speaker has said. If a statement is not clear to somebody, he or she may tell the speaker, "I didn't quite understand what you meant; can you say it another way?" or "Is there more you would like to say about that?" Note that this is simply a request for clarification and is not to be used as an excuse to judge or criticize the speaker's communication.

If you want to follow the usual three-process format (e.g., Nurturing–Clearing–Affirming), we recommend that you break up into small groups of three to five and allow yourselves at least 30 minutes for completion. If you want to have a Heart-to-Heart Talk with a large group of more than five people at once and have only a limited amount of time, we recommend that you select one process only, a Nurturing Process. (Remember never to use a Clearing or Discovery Process without following it up with a Nurturing or Affirming Process.)

NURTURING PROCESSES

Something I like about you is...

Something I respect about you is...

Something I admire about you is...

Something I love about you is...

Something I would like to be acknowledged for is...

Something I would like to acknowledge you for is...

Something I am thankful for is...

Something I love in my life is...

One of the happiest times I have had with you is...

Something I am good at is...

Something I feel good about is...

Something I would like to experience more with you is...

One of the ways I like to express my love is...

One of the ways I like to be loved is...

CLEARING PROCESSES

Something I am concerned about is...

Something I need to say is...

Something I have been afraid to tell you is...

Something that irritates me is...

Something I think you should know is...

A feeling I've been having is...

One of my fears about doing these processes is...

One of my fears about continuing these processes is...

EXAMPLES OF RESPONSES IN A CLEARING PROCESS TO BOND WITH FAMILY

A feeling I've been having is...

- that you didn't like it when I decided to take the semester off from college.

- you want me to pitch in more with the housework.

- boredom and restlessness.

- you're upset with me about something, but I don't know what.

- I'm wondering if we should move.

- everyone is walking on eggshells.

DISCOVERY PROCESSES

Something I like about my family is...

Something I think supports a happy home is...

Something I would like for you to know about me is...

Something I have always wanted in my family is...

Something that would improve our family is...

Something I would like to change in my family is...

Something I want in my family relationships is...

Something that's difficult for me in family relationships is...

Something that interferes with a happy home is...

Something that is difficult with parents is...

Something that is difficult with children is...

Something that is difficult with family members is...

Something that is important to me in my family is...

Something I don't want in my family relationships is...

Something I am afraid of in family relationships is...

 AFFIRMING PROCESSES

Your true thoughts and feelings are important.

You are a valuable and appreciated member of this family.

You deserve to be respected and listened to.

It's safe and rewarding for you to ask for what you want.

The more love you give the more love you receive, and the more love you receive the more love you give.

Our family is strong, and we are protected by our love.

Please feel free to make up your own.

CHAPTER ELEVEN

ENHANCING
TIES WITH CO-WORKERS

Without a doubt, one of the richest yet most overlooked possibilities for human connection is our relationships with the people in our workplace. Despite spending eight or more hours a day with our co-workers, they are often strangers to us, as everyone focuses on job responsibilities and the tasks of running a business. It adds up to a lot of missed opportunities.

There is no time like the present to initiate a Heart-to-Heart Talk in your office or business environment. These processes lay much-needed groundwork for opening up the channels of communication, resolving personality conflicts, ensuring that everyone is heard, and strengthening people's sense of unity, teamwork, and camaraderie. Not only can problems be solved in this way, but through the regular use of Heart-to-Heart Talks, they can be prevented or minimized in the first place.

Heart-to-Heart Talks with co-workers can be done one-on-one or in a group setting. We suggest that everyone sit around a table and take turns in a circle until everyone has had a chance to speak. The same guidelines that were given in the previous chapter apply here: A special object is passed from speaker to speaker to signify whose turn it is. Listeners should nod silently rather than respond verbally after each statement, unless they need to ask for clarification. If time is limited, a large group of more than five people should either break up into smaller groups to do a three-process format, or do only one process (preferably a Nurturing Process) as an entire group. In any case, a Clearing or Discovery Process should not be used unless it can be followed with a Nurturing or Affirming Process.

NURTURING PROCESSES

Something I like about you is...

Something I respect about you is...

Something I admire about you is...

Something I love about you is...

Something I would like to be acknowledged for is...

Something I would like to acknowledge you for is...

Something I am thankful for is...

Something I love in my life is...

One of the happiest times I have had with you is...

Something I am good at is...

Something I feel good about is...

Something I would like to experience more with you is...

CLEARING PROCESSES

Something I am concerned about is...

Something I need to say is...

Something I have been afraid to tell you is...

Something that irritates me is...

Something I think you should know is...

A feeling I've been having is...

One of my fears about doing these processes is...

One of my fears about continuing these processes is...

DISCOVERY PROCESSES

Something I like about my job is...

Something I like about my company is...

Something I like about my profession is...

Something I think supports a positive workplace is...

Something I would like for you to know about me is...

Something I have always wanted in my career is...

Something I want in my business/professional relationships is...

Something that's difficult for me in business/professional relationships is...

Something I would like to change or improve in my job is...

Something that would improve our company is...

Something that interferes with a positive workplace is...

Something that is difficult at work is...

Something that is important to me in my job is...

Something that is important to me in my company is...

Something that is important to me in my profession is...

Something I don't want in business/professional relationships is...

Something I am afraid of in business/professional relationships is...

EXAMPLES OF RESPONSES IN A DISCOVERY PROCESS WITH CO-WORKERS

Something I would like to change or improve in my job is...

- the level of communication between everybody.
- to find some way of keeping the meetings shorter and more on track.
- being able to give constructive feedback without being afraid I'm hurting someone's feelings.
- getting more timely performance reviews.
- having a more specific job function.
- boosting morale in general.

AFFIRMING PROCESSES

You have everything it takes to succeed with people.

Your true thoughts and feelings are important.

It is safe and rewarding for you to ask for what you really want.

You are a valuable contribution to this company, and everyone sees it.

Your creative ideas are welcomed and appreciated here.

People admire, respect, and support you.

Please feel free to make up your own.

$\mathscr{C}$HAPTER TWELVE

CREATING
LOVE AND ROMANCE

Romantic love—the passionate and sublime union of souls that brings human beings closest to embracing a spark of the divine—can be life's greatest adventure. The intensity of feeling that people have for their beloved can lift them to the greatest heights, or plunge them to the lowest depths, for they have an incredible amount of emotion invested in their ideas of what a successful romantic relationship should look and feel like.

True love can certainly start with a well-timed kiss and a ride into the sunset, but it takes more to live happily ever after. In the twenty years we've been working with individuals and couples, we've seen one factor more than any other spell the success or failure of a love relationship: the couple's ongoing quality of communication. Heart-to-Heart Talks like the ones in this chapter formed the foundation of our own romantic relationship. Whether you are beginning a new romance, or trying to make a good marriage even better, or seeking to renew and revitalize a relationship you've been in for many years, you can use these processes to enjoy immediate and profound results.

NURTURING PROCESSES

Something I like about you is...

Something I respect about you is...

Something I admire about you is...

Something I love about you is...

One of the ways I like to express my love is...

One of the ways I like to be loved is...

Something I like about myself is...

Something that makes me happy is...

Something I love in my life is...

Being in love is important because...

One of the happiest times I have had with you is...

I like being in love with you because...

Something I would like to experience more with you is...

EXAMPLES OF RESPONSES IN A
NURTURING PROCESS TO CREATE LOVE & ROMANCE

I like being in love with you because...

- ❧ you bring out the best in me.
- ❧ I love to give to you, and you're so easy to give to.
- ❧ it makes me so happy!
- ❧ I feel like you respect me for who I am, not some idealized image.
- ❧ you make my heart sing!
- ❧ I love to hold you and gaze into your eyes.
- ❧ together we can move mountains.

CLEARING PROCESSES

Something I am concerned about is...

Something I need to say is...

Something I have been afraid to tell you is...

Something that irritates me is...

Something I think you should know is...

A feeling I have been having is...

One of my fears about doing these processes is...

One of my fears about continuing these processes is...

DISCOVERY PROCESSES

Something I like about men is...

Something I like about women is...

Something I like about sex is...

Something I have always wanted to do is...

If I felt sexier I would...

If I felt more loved I would...

Something that needs to happen for me to feel loved and appreciated is...

Something that needs to happen for me to feel sexually satisfied is...

Something I would like to change or improve in my marriage is...

Something I want in my romantic relationships is...

Something that's difficult for me in romantic relationships is...

Something I would like to change or improve in my/our romantic relationship(s) is...

One of the ways I know I can trust someone is...

What happens for me when I stop trusting is...

Something that confuses me about romantic love is...

Something that confuses me about sex is...

Something that confuses me about men is...

Something that confuses me about women is...

Something that confuses me about marriage is...

I resist commitments because...

Something I don't want in my romantic relationships is...

Something I am afraid of in romantic relationships is...

Something I am afraid of in sex is...

Something that scares me about intimacy is...

One of the ways I avoid intimacy is...

Something that is important to me in marriage is...

Something that is important to me in my/our romantic relationship(s) is...

AFFIRMING PROCESSES

You deserve a life filled with romance and passion.

You are an exciting, desirable lover.

Our life is overflowing with love and romance.

Our love is growing deeper in tenderness and beauty every day.

We show our love for each other frequently throughout each day.

We deserve to have our relationship exactly the way we want it.

Please feel free to make up your own.

CHAPTER THIRTEEN
SHARING
POWER AND CO-CREATION

From what we've seen in the past several years, human beings are in the process of making an evolutionary leap in the way they deal with power. The old paradigm of using power to control and dominate is giving way to a new paradigm of cooperation and co-creation. In this new paradigm there is an appreciation for our interconnectedness and an honoring of our differences. We have a new commitment to finding ways of living harmoniously and sharing power to co-create living situations that benefit each unique individual as well as the whole.

To do this we need to overcome the prejudices born of fear and ignorance. Some of the greatest inequities in the use of power are in the area of gender and racial differences. Many of us have been harmed by the abuse of power, and we need to forgive others for their ignorance. We need to heal these hurts and claim our own power. Some of us have been held back so much that we need to give ourselves permission to discover and ask for what we really want and need. Sometimes we need to lend a helping hand, and sometimes we need to allow ourselves to be newly encouraged and supported.

You will note that a few of the processes are designed to focus on a specific group of your choice. Select one group, and one group only, for the duration of the process. For example, if you start with, "Something I respect about people who are Black is... ", don't switch to Latino, Asian-American, or anyone else. Finish the group you started out with. Then, if you wish, you may repeat the process with a different group of individuals, as many times as you want.

NURTURING PROCESSES

Something I like about powerful people (men, women, other groups) is...

Something I like about being powerful is...

Something I like about men is...

Something I like about women is...

Something I respect about (people who are Black, Latino, Catholic, gay, Caucasian, democrat, etc.) is...

Something I like about you is...

Something I respect about you is...

Something I admire about you is...

Something I love about you is...

Something I would like to be acknowledged for is...

Something I would like to acknowledge you for is...

Something I am thankful for is...

Something I love in my life is...

One of the happiest times I have had with you is...

Something I am good at is...

Something I feel good about is...

Something I would like to experience more with you is...

EXAMPLES OF RESPONSES
IN A NURTURING PROCESS
TO SHARE POWER AND CO-CREATION

Something I love in my life is...

- weekends.

- saxophone music.

- the way the air smells after it rains.

- the softness of puppies.

- watching a beautiful sunset.

- dancing.

- popcorn and parades!

CLEARING PROCESSES

One of my fears of being powerful is...

Powerful people (men, women, other groups) make me feel...

One of my concerns about powerful people (men, women, other groups) is...

One of the ways I have abused power in the past is...

One of the ways I have been abused in the past is...

Something I need to say about power is...

My fear of letting go of control is...

Something I have been afraid to tell you is...

Something that irritates me is...

One of my fears about doing these processes is...

One of my fears about continuing these processes is...

Something I think you should know is...

A feeling I have been having is...

DISCOVERY PROCESSES

I hold back my power because...

I hold back my true opinions because...

One of the ways I hold myself back is...

One of my fears of asking for what I really want is...

Sharing power with others is easy because...

Sharing power with others is difficult because...

When others disagree with me I feel...

Something I would like for you to know about me is...

Something I want in my relationships is...

Something that's difficult for me in relationships is...

Something I don't want in my relationships is...

Something I am afraid of in relationships is...

I have to be in control because...

To be more powerful I would have to...

AFFIRMING PROCESSES

Your power is safe for everyone.

You wield your power wisely and safely.

You are safe in the presence of powerful people.

People want you to be powerful.

It is safe for you to be revealed as a powerful person.

The people you love want you to be powerful.

Others are safe when you are powerful.

You always express your power in safe and appropriate ways.

It is safe for you to trust male power.

It is safe for you to trust female power.

It is safe and rewarding for you to share your power equally with (men, women, other groups).

You can allow others to be powerful without feeling diminished.

You can trust yourself in the presence of others' power.

You can be in the presence of power without relinquishing authority.

You are respected even when others disagree with you.

Please feel free to make up your own.

CHAPTER FOURTEEN

WINDOWS OF
THE SOUL

It is said that the eyes are the windows of the soul. We all have the ability to pour our love out of our eyes and focus it on someone. We all likewise have the ability to receive love through our eyes simply by meeting the gaze of the one who is loving us and consciously breathing deeply, allowing love into our body, mind, and heart. Although this can be frightening for some (love brings up anything unlike itself, remember?), it can be a powerfully healing and transforming experience. As our capacity for giving and receiving love grows, it takes only a minute of total focus and openness to reestablish a connection with someone. It does take practice, however, and that's what this process is for.

As in the other processes, sit across from one another and get comfortable. Determine in advance who will be the giver and who will be the receiver. When you are the giver, allow your gaze to rest gently on the face and eyes of your partner. Imagine you have a dial on your heart that is like the aperture of a camera, and you can open and close it at will. Now you are going to practice opening it to let as much love flow out of you as possible. In your imagination, connect that flow of love from your heart to your eyes, and let it pour out of your eyes into those of your partner. Remember to keep breathing as you do this, with long, slow, deep breaths, in and out.

When you are the receiver, likewise allow your gaze to rest gently on the face and eyes of your partner. Your job is to open your heart and mind, and breathe in the love your partner is sending you. Open the aperture of your heart to let in as much love as you want. If you begin to feel that it is getting too intense and you want to avert your gaze, "stretch" yourself into the love even more. Then, if you wish, you may simply close your eyes and just be with the feelings. You may open your eyes again when you are ready.

In the beginning you should time this process just as you do the others. When the two minutes are up, switch and allow the giver to receive love while the receiver now practices giving it. Before long you will find that the distinction between giving

Breathe in the love your partner is sending you.

and receiving disappears in the timeless flow of love between the two of you.

It is very important that you pay attention to your breath in this process—and indeed in all the others. One of the ways we all unconsciously brace ourselves against love is by shallow breathing or actually holding our breath. One of the best things to do is breathe deeply and pretend you are breathing the love into you. If your body starts to feel tingly at all, take deeper, slower breaths.

When you become more proficient with this process, your capacity to give and receive love will take a quantum leap. This expanded ability will, in turn, become normal and natural—an ever-present part of your life.

CHAPTER FIFTEEN

A NEW WAY
OF LIVING

You have embarked on a marvelous journey, the adventure of the heart. This is only the beginning.

Whatever it was that brought you to this book—earnest curiosity, a desire to communicate more effectively with others, the pain of a broken relationship, the persistent feeling that there must be more to life—the truth is now that you've taken the first steps on this path of healing, there is no turning back.

Opening up your heart takes immense courage. By initiating Heart-to-Heart Talks with people you want to know better or people you already care deeply about, you have created a place for learning, growing, and healing—an unlimited space of possibilities.

You have entered the realm of Evolutionary Relationships.

Evolutionary Relationships is a term we have coined to distinguish relationships that are committed to personal and spiritual evolution, for both the individual and the human species. People who create Evolutionary Relationships are focused on having relationships that reflect purposeful action rooted in love. These are people who want to bring out the best in themselves and others. They want to bring forth their wisest and most loving aspects, using that resource for the betterment of humanity. These are people who have said goodbye to the old ways of using power over others abusively, no longer indulging in adversarial attitudes or behaviors. They have recognized an interconnectedness among all life and have pledged to honor it by seeking solutions that work for everyone. They have made a commitment to rise above their own fears and complaints and to focus their creative powers on generating positive action.

Clearly, this is no small endeavor. But can there be a more noble and practical pursuit? How would your life be different if each day you asked yourself, "Who made my choices today— fear or love?"

Consciously creating Evolutionary Relationships requires impeccability and a new level of honesty with yourself. It means viewing the world through new eyes and striving to maintain the ongoing "conversation" that promotes nurturing, clearing, discovery, and affirming. Perhaps it requires weekly or even daily

Evolutionary Relationships are committed to personal and spiritual evolution.

Heart-to-Heart Talks with some of the people in your life. For others, it may mean simply broaching the possibility of a Heart-to-Heart Talk, or giving them a copy of this book so they may become acquainted with it at their own pace. We wrote *Straight From the Heart* to serve not only as a resource but also an invitation. As such, it is ideally suited as a gift for your friends, co-workers, and family members. What could be better than to invite your loved ones to join you on this new path of learning, growing, and healing?

Another extraordinary opportunity is to form ongoing study groups. Can you imagine what it would be like to meet with a group of committed people on a regular basis to do these processes and to share with one another what happens? We strongly encourage you to assume responsibility for initiating such a study group as an experiment. You can form a study group from among your friends, family, co-workers, or church group. The ideal number of people to work with are from four to twelve. It's a good idea to have a stopwatch and time each process for two minutes, selecting someone to be timekeeper.

No doubt as you've begun to use these processes, you've experienced intense emotions. Perhaps you've noticed things immediately starting to get better. Perhaps you've also noticed a host of bewildering feelings rising to the surface, sensations you're not quite sure what to do about. Don't deny these feelings or try to stuff them back down. Don't make more of them than they really are, either. Just feel them, and *let them pass*. Anger may turn into confusion which may turn into sadness which may turn into something else. Let it pass.

You may also find that this book ignites a powerful desire in you that you didn't even know existed—a thirst for new dimensions of human experience, a hunger to give and create and go farther than you ever have before. Trust in yourself, and trust in the healing power of love.

$\mathcal{M}$ORE RESOURCES FROM HEART TO HEART

We lovingly offer the following products as an enrichment to your life and relationships.

STRAIGHT FROM THE HEART— POWER TOOLS FOR EVOLUTIONARY RELATIONSHIPS

The companion to the book you have just read is a set of six audio tapes and a workbook. The tapes are tools for transforming your beliefs and attitudes to help you create your relationships exactly the way you want them.

Six Cassettes and Workbook $90

SCREAMING PILLOW

The "screaming pillows" mentioned in Part One of this book (page 39) are specially designed and made with baffles and batting to absorb sound. They're ideal for expressing your anger in a safe and appropriate way.

Pillow (Portable Size) $15

SECRETS FOR SUCCESSFUL RELATIONSHIPS HOME-STUDY MANUAL AND AUDIO TAPE

We present a comprehensive, two-part curriculum called "Secrets for Successful Relationships" in San Diego, California, which is delivered over three weekends and totals more than 60 hours. To make this material more immediately accessible, we offer you this special-edition home-study course. And to familiarize you further with Heart to Heart, our "Secrets" audio tape gives you a taste of what the workshop would be like if you attended in person.

Workbook $95

Audio Tape $10

To order products and to learn how you can attend "Secrets for Successful Relationships" in person, please call (800) 500-LOVE (5683) or write to us at the address below.

We would love to hear from you! Please write to us with your stories of success, breakthroughs, and miracles.

Heart to Heart
7720-B El Camino Real
Suite 441
La Costa, CA 92009
(619) 436-8844
HTH_NOW@aol.com

All products are fully guaranteed, so in the unlikely event you are not satisfied, you can send them back for a full refund, minus shipping and handling.